Lost Citizen

Selected Poems
1995–2003

William Gillespie

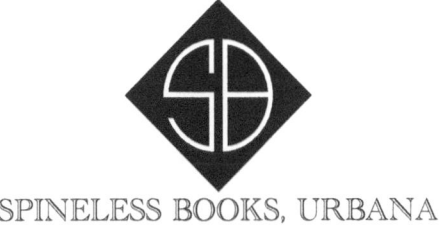

SPINELESS BOOKS, URBANA

Contents

Dedication

For, after, with, because of
Stephanie Strickland

Osculate

My pulse kept awake
Imagine a hand, a mile of darkness
Carbonated heart, shaken
Incomprehensible, pleasurable
Close your eyes, navigate the mirror maze
Fractured syntax where two curves touch
Calculate together their most accurate tangent

Bring every nerve into writhing life
Define interior and exterior space
To map, two continents dance
Every contour etched by flame
Your skin a sail filled with wind
Your eyes shut open
Your mouth inside out
You burn like a match

Static of Baghdad

so

does the cocktail pianist strafe the piano full of smoking holes?
the screaming will again dissolve in static, noise = too much
information
the language to describe these catastrophes, these deaths, is
written with an alphabet unfamiliar to us
the music likewise does not sound like a language to us;
unfamiliar scales, alphabets. we tear out the pages we
cannot read
whatever sentiment is illegible and unintelligible to us. the
word for chemical weapon is different, we would not be
able to tell it from the word for "grandmother" or "hospital"

but

Bush pronounced Sad*dam Sad*dam. they are two different
words. one denotes royalty, the other peasantry. how did
Bush pronounce the word when it referred to our ally,
ruthless dictator notwithstanding
strangers in a night lit by pinpoint accuracy
an eye for an eye. one eye for the other eye. they are our eyes
write a letter to a congressperson, a letter from another
alphabet. the twentyseventh letter. write them something
they had been unable to think before you did
every time you scream and shout it sounds like harmony
for example, this is a better country to homosexuals and
women, if you can imagine a worse country

if

you can imagine it noon in the desert and perfectly dark and
    starving men weeping in a marketplace without water, if
    you can imagine unbelievable prosperity stolen by its own
    marketplace, if you can watch the evening news seeing only
    that which is not shown, if you can imagine pinpoint
    accuracy of the cameras not the bombs
selfappointed middlemanagement of the world
ouch
there is a certain ineluctable machinery, there is this human
    nature, there is inevitable justice, there is an invisible hand,
    there has to be an invisible sun, we are the world, we are
so it tells us

    or

a world in which depletable resources are, simply, not resources
a world without women, men, veils, ties
in which language is purified by water, wind
people become excited when they find an old Pepsi can, proof
    of the otherwise unbelievable history before the rise of the
    cogs

    the piano shoots first

the pianist will learn to speak in the key
the A major alphabet: A C E F H J L M
and in A minor he learns to speak as well:
A C D F H I L M
it is now midnight and the marketplace is lit by flickering
    clouds and noise
they line up with uncrumpled papercups where the gutter
drips in the smoke

a world when

bullets are so rare nobody would ever dream of firing
people are so valuable nobody would even dream of
the individual nations are as valuable as the minutes on the
    clock
the sun passes through each every day, horizon denotes a
    movement
there are piccolos in the treetops and tubas in the woods at
    night
there is interesting food and thus language

      now

wake up tomorrow determined not to bomb anything,
    determined, absolutely determined
remember, too, that everything you write comes true and is
    delicious
remember to write
wake up or determine anything, *determine*, absolutely
    determine that everything you write comes true and is
tomorrow wake up and discover that this is your world and
    was all along (at the forum he said democracy was a state
    when the poor, getting the upper hand, kill off the
    aristocrats and divide up their wealth, usually by drawing
    lots, it is when a mountain of confusion accumulates the
    first pebble, and a garden grows wild around the first petal:
    speech), climb the garden, wander the mountain

4

With Shoes Like These

I will walk over buildings of arches and gilding with shoes like
these like these. I will stalk through the mist with my doctors
assisting with shoes like these with shoes. I will run like a
thunderstorm rend streets asunder with shoes like these
with these. Preparing for anarchy barnstorm the lock key
with shoes like these with like. Testdrive survival for culture's
revival with shoes like these shoes like. Get so much stronger
with legs so much longer with shoes like these shoes these.

Poem for Money III:
Light Fuse and Get Away

Oh no not again
They haven't healed as quickly as I'd hoped
I can't wear long sleeves it's 101 degrees
In order to boost seratonin levels
You need a job
Which also releases gas-pedal chemicals into the brain such as
Vending machine coffee

See what I mean? Before
I could even finish the stanza
I had to spend my last $200
Rent or food, on a lost catfight
Maybe it wasn't lost, I mean
How much were the other cat's bills?
Never mind
Hey, wait, listen:
How is it possible for me to worry about
Personal debt and global nuclear war since
Only one of the two can happen?

This summer is an economic roller coaster
Lose two jobs get one. Well
Roller coasters go up and down
I guess it's an economic subway
Which starts and stops and lurches
And makes me sick

I'm not depressed, I'm—
Well, okay, maybe I'm depressed

But

I'm still employable

Right?

July 1ˢᵗ, 1998

$1000

Ha, ha, just kidding

But seriously, $.59 or so, anyhow

What made me think I could afford to own cats?
Or teeth? Or feet? Or a stomach?

I mean, look at it this way

If you do not pay this amount by July 1st
Your coverage will be cancelled

When it is rephrased in these terms
Certain deeper meanings surface

Staying in bed all day, every day
Makes certain things possible
How long would it take, for example, to read
All my books in alphabetic order?

At the rate I buy them, this was
Once impossible

Sorry, bought, but now

And my father said, remember this
If you are going to amass real wealth
You have to become a stock market investor

I guess that makes this a novel
According to one of the only two things
We remember about Bakhtin

Polyglossia and using old manuscripts
To roll tobacco
When he couldn't afford paper. But he also
Had an idea. But me

In the sport of basketball
The importance of scoring points
Cannot be underestimated

So you see what I'm up against

No, really, why do I have such a hard time
Critiquing capitalism on an empty stomach

THIN: *Ribs easily palpable with minimal fat covering;*
Lumbar vertebrae obvious; obvious
Waist behind ribs; minimal abdominal fat.

Print "you have $cash bucks\n";

Anyhow, this is not that
I lost as many as four friends in one week
And may cause health problems
Never mind, on the positive side, I'm
Writing this at least

Yeah, well
The position for which you applied
Has been filled by an internal applicant
Who
We feel will best meet our needs

Best wishes for future success

Thank you for helping to make affirmative action work

Little Villainelle

Wearing just explosives, Venus in the Shell
Station and she's sweetly asking for the till
Give the bastards hell my little Villainelle

Gentle curl of copper burning in farewell
Winks from her tiara, leaves without the bill
Wearing just explosives, Venus in the Shell

Billows golden flame, it silences the yell
Dust all glitters falling, everything is still
Give the bastards hell my little Villainelle

Burning what they're giving, stealing what they sell
Silver plumed exhaust, it burns across the hill
Wearing just explosives, Venus in the Shell

Where the smoke will rise, no thinker can foretell
Frightened of all poems, they suppress the thrill
Give the bastards hell my little Villainelle

Prop the exit open, disconnect the bell
Give her what she wants and no excuse to kill
Wearing just explosives, Venus in the Shell
Give the bastards hell my little Villainelle

Pursumi

your prose breeze eases
the ebb and flow of windy
crisis, steadyslow

lighthouse candlefire
the match head erupts in flame
and you shine and I

Newspoem 5 January 1995

When AT&T announced its intentions to lay off 40,000 workers, the shit really hit the fan. Those Wall Street analysts who applauded the job trimming were pretty surprised when 40,000 AT&T workers showed up in their neighborhoods to dismantle their houses and cars in a matter of minutes. You should have seen them storm the company's headquarters. They really fucked shit up: it wasn't pretty. The thousand meter high neon acronym whitened the sky with showers of sparks as 40,000 AT&T workers dragged it from its foundations. When they sang their song in 40,000-part harmony it drove bats crazy and coastguard ships collided with oil tankers. It sure didn't take 40,000 AT&T workers long to rip down every telephone cable from Newark to New Brunswick. 40,000 is a lot of disgruntled AT&T workers, especially when compared to a leap in the Dow Jones Industrial Average of a measly 60 points. What if 40,000 angry AT&T workers got together with 3000 furious MCI employees, 5000 screaming General Motors employees, and 22,000 pissed Times-Mirror employees? They could do a lot of damage pretty quickly, especially when some of them are entitled to healthcare for an additional year.

Transmiss

The rest of the week stretches before me like
This morning I threw up for no reason that I can
The ladies don't bother saying hi to me anymore and I
If I won the lottery I would work harder than
I should be able to come up with a more profound
Maybe I should just never leave this
They've stopped inviting me to meetings too because
I have wrapped myself in a cocoon of silence so
If I were a better lover I'd
Why have I spent all my
I tried to put paintings on the wall but the wall
I used to try to listen to music but
The hum of the dehumidifiers is like
I am an animal in a cage, one that nobody wants to
After work I will just
No substances of any kind, even food, have
Damn it all to

What else can I do, I'm wearing this stupid striped short-
    sleeved
They are all women, so they are sexist to men, because
As if I am a metonymy for every man who ever
There is much too much I'd rather
Even this miserable poem is a violation of the Protestant
With each day I get more alienated, more entrenched, but
They all hate me or maybe I hate
It's all bad, or so it seems to me, right
I am a human ghetto or so I feel in this
And nothing will help, no shirt, sobriety, or

It took you to make my house so big and empty, some
I'm paying rent on air and
There's probably nothing we can
No, there's nothing we can
After all, it's October and

The Week The News Was Put in Prison

20 March 1996

The News would regret the day it ever wrote about a prison system. Its own News was fast becoming far too real. Finding that comet had been a brilliant move that happened too late. Four guards came to arrest The News at midnight. It was submitted to proofreading—a degrading procedure—and put in solitary confinement.

21 March 1996

Throughout the day, the other periodicals screamed for matches, cigarettes, toilet paper, sang eerie songs, made speeches, and yelled at each other to shut up. The food was a very small black-and-white photograph of what appeared to be cabbage in cream sauce. The News could not see the comet from within its eight-by-eleven cell.

22 March 1996

The sewers backed up and The News huddled on its wooden bench trembling, watching the excrement wash by across the concrete floor. For the first time it was led into the general prison population, afraid it would be recognized. Gigantic prisoners approached it carrying old newspapers, pointed to graphs of rising crime rates and articles about the need for more prisons, and said, "Remember me?"

23 March 1996

The News, dozing in its cell, was beaten with a bag of padlocks and stabbed twice by assailants who held a pillow over its face. The News was taped together without anesthetic and put back in solitary.

24 March 1996

The News could no longer follow the presidential primaries. The News had no idea how the election in Taiwan turned out. The News had a tiny radio for a while and on headsets it could listen to Rush Limbaugh complain about the easy life of prisoners. The batteries slowly died replacing the signal with noise. The excrement scrawled across the cement.

25 March 1996

The day The News was executed I went to reclaim its possessions, which consisted of a single handgun. Back home I took a screwdriver and removed a panel from its side. Inside was an entire typewriter. An amazing trick of concealment. Its entire week on death row, The News had had a typewriter the whole time, but never used it. It must have had a plan to lower the crime rate, end the death penalty, and rehabilitate prisoners; a plan which it decided not to execute. With the comet nearing perihelion our nights are now bathed in a green glow. This has made the streets safe and reading at night possible.

Conjecture and Proposition

So my husband comes first and the marriage after
But my husband stays between
Nor does he admit what lurks beneath
And the marriage can't give me up
Or I will let it down
So I propose that I spend some time alone with my
    relationship with the marriage and discuss what lurks
    below
But my husband gets nervous and doesn't want his relationship
    with my relationship with the marriage to change or
    exclude him or be over
Nor does he want to admit what lurks below the ground he
    stands upon
And whenever he goes away for two weeks and leaves me alone
    with the marriage and I retile and wash and wax the floor
    and am happy it's funny how he only misses me when I
    don't miss him and point it out
Or even when I just try to take a day off

So my marriage and I are running away from my husband
    together

A Glossary of Poetic Abstraction

FIDELITY (fi*del*i*ty) 1. Sound quality of stereo components. 2. The state of monogamy, whether explicit or not.

> *A chessboard in a forest. A woman in a white dress sits at one side of the chessboard, waiting for another player. Knights ride by on snorting white steeds, armor clanking. They avoid eyecontact as they ride by. One of them notes that she is in check. She is sad but patient. She waits for someone to stop and take her king so that she can be out of the game forever.*

DEMOCRACY (he*ge*mon*y) 1. In ancient Greece a form of patriarchy. 2. Rule by an elected official & 10,000 armed policemen.

> *A circle of people. They take turns speaking for five minutes each. They each speak a different language and nobody understands what anybody else says. Furthermore, each measures minutes differently. One of them thinks a minute is the length of time it takes Jupiter to revolve around the sun—88 years. None of them know what they are gathered there to discuss.*

FAMILY VALUES (wel*fare*cut) 1. A Reagan/Bushism concealing a particular domestic agenda. Married homosexual couples raising children are not considered families. Single mothers are not considered families. Neighbors are not considered families. Neighboring countries are not considered families. Families of species are not considered families. Most importantly, the country and everyone in it is not considered a family.

> *Donald Trump and Bill Gates stare into one another's eyes dreamily above the candles, wineglasses, tablecloth. Bill puts his hand on Donald's. Bill is about to say something important. The violinist senses this and drifts to another table. But the waiter has arrived tableside carrying a television set on a silver platter. The government policies you ordered have arrived, gentlemen, it is time for the president's state of the union address. They turn their chairs to face the traytable as the waiter pulls the foil off of the neck of the frosted bottle and prepares to uncork the champagne.*

KITTENHOOD or KITTENNESS (kyoot)
1. [undefinable]

> *La Maga is stalking a butterfly. She is the color of cappuccino-vanilla swirl ice cream. The butterfly is red, the grass is green, the sky is blue. She runs halfway up a tree, jumps off, runs to another tree, climbs halfway up.*

TRUTH (pow*er) 1. The truth. 2. A lie.

Galileo is squinting through a telescope at a piece of green cheese in the heavens. He stands up and replaces the lens. He bends to look into the eyepiece again. He is now looking straight into the eye of God who is Catholic and furious. He stands up and replaces the lens, bends to look into the eyepiece again. He sees a rabbit. He makes a note on some parchment. He replaces the lens, bends. This time he sees a woman with a water pitcher. He smiles.

BEAUTY (pow*er*fail*ure) 1. That quality which, when possessed, makes a person, place, thing, or idea beautiful.

The branches of the sapling fork like the crack in the brick wall.
The crack in the brick wall angles like the fork of lightning in the prairie.
The fork of lightning in the prairie is as angular as the spiderweb in the bathroom.
The spiderweb in the bathroom radiates like the cracks in the shattered windshield.
The cracks in the windshield are the same cracks as the cracks in the ice on the pond.
The cracks in the ice on the pond resemble the fractures in the skull on the x-ray.
The line on the electroencephalocardiograph is as flat as the horizon where the lightning struck before the car hit the tree.
Nobody has been back to his apartment since.

CRUELTY (un*em*ploy*ment*com*pen*sa*tion*can*celled)
1. Not noticing or not caring.

> *The one whose job it is to refuse healthcare to people who are unemployed is at the hospital cafeteria. She has just quit her job. When she requests a refill on her coffee, holding out her cup across the counter, the woman behind the counter pours the coffee, calmly and deliberately, onto the wrist of the person whose job it was to refuse healthcare to those who are unemployed. The person screams and jerks her hand away, sending her elbow through the glass window of a cooler in which pies are displayed. Her arm is mangled and bloody and she is screaming with rage and pain. The woman behind the counter shrugs. Her daughter cannot afford healthcare.*

MORALITY (mar*ket) 1. Generally morality is conceived as a market, generally with acts thought to be kind or just or selfless or merely difficult conceived of as profit, and acts that are selfish, corrupt, hypocritical, or forbidden conceived of as expenditure. This is only one of the many ways in which morality is conceived or talked about, but it is prevalent in our culture. For example:

> "Having done my good deed for the day, I treated myself to an ice-cream cone."

> "Since I had let him borrow the rake, I figured that it was okay if I took his lawnmower without asking."

> "It didn't bother me that I was sleeping with his wife. It's not like he was a very good husband."

> *I am looking at you. You are far away. Beneath us is a convoluted maze whose geometry sprawls to the edge of vision. I can't swallow. Do we both know the maze is there?*

> *I look up and see we are each standing in the pans of a large scale. We are opposite each other and weigh approximately the same. When I try to move, the scale shifts and I see you lose your balance, grabbing a chain for support.*

Assignment

I know I'm going to get in trouble for starting this, and someone should take away my poetic license. But I got a job with the postalservice so I could stop by your house. Would you move to a different zone? Tell me quickly for it is almost winter. The North Pole is really dark this time of year. Even the snow is black. There are only a few things I know how to do and identifying them is not one of them. I have categories for everything. Let me give you an example: matchbooks with a single match torn out are in a different category than unopened matchbooks, which are in the same category as unopened books. I have a lot of those. I don't know what I'll do if I don't find a reader soon. Swoon. Or drop into the snow, an angel. I got a letter in the mail that began "Dear Steak Enthusiast." This is intimacy. There are too many things to elaborate on. If I thought you'd finish this page I'd finish it too. What a wonderful world that would be. Harry Mathews says that the creative act is done by the reader, the writer providing the tools. Paul Auster, similarly, cautions against overdescription in fiction. I don't know what to believe myself. One or the other probably doesn't exist—reader or writer—in any event there is some imagination which takes place up upon a balcony overlooking a Renaissance stage from seats padded with straw. Is anybody listening? Of course someone is. I have no one to write to. Tell me about it. End of paragraph. Okay let me cut to the quick, the chase, if you will, as it were, and get down to brass tacks, business: Writing is a way of Being. That's all. It is, as Auster writes, not a profession one chooses: it chooses you. Echoing on this point Mathews who thinks that the only less-rewarding profession must be being a musician, as musicians require organized performances, whereas the writer can whisper to a captive audience in the privacy of a bedroom or subway car. Then comes the hunger, but, to look on the bright side, that hunger may well have come anyway. So think of yourself as a railroad conductor instead. Constant motion in a direction. Like arrows, vectors, rays. Like light, sound, grammar, narrative, melody. Like telephone wires over hillsides, the lines rise and fall together. There is no one to tell these things to. If I tell these things to an empty forest will a tree fall and if so will I exist or will that confirm that the world is a hallucination, an imaginative projection. Fancy. Or was it folly. But to get back on track to my point, I would encourage you to correct the chaos of your life one element at a time, tireless and methodical and determined, think of it as failing to lose ground, a very slow and determined effort. Direction is good but not necessary as is clear from examining the motions of a butterfly. I would have called you to tell you these things but I'm not sure you would have understood the gesture. I'd fax it to you if I could, but let's be reasonable, you don't even use email. Why should you? How could you? I am, however, strictly speaking, a treasure trove of potentially interesting advice. Next time you balance your checkbook, write a line of poetry for every check, with one word for every dollar spent. Next time there is trouble with the bowels, you may write a long line on toilet paper proceeding lengthwise. It is like this. Every postcard you mail off becomes a patch in the quilt, a cloud in the sky, until all is opaque and there comes a sudden wind or cloudburst. It's autumn: try not to pass up this chance to be melancholy. It is precisely the right temperature for the mind, and it is like thought or weather fleeting and indeterminate, despite efforts to fix the temperature at a single number at a fictional instant in time and space, or efforts to count the number of words per line. Also, you might want to write a poem for every item on your grocery list and tape them up in the store. An anthology of your best writing can only be organized so many ways, but a grocery store is a landscape of shifting categories for charcoal, lightbulbs, and vegetarian meat. Then, when you write the poems for the grocery store, lift weights with your left hand and write with your right or the other way around. For every repetition write a letter to Patch

24

Adams or State Representative Johnson or me. Then write a poem on the outside of the envelope, xerox the envelope, copy the poem onto a cocktail napkin at a crowded sports bar during Happy Hour (IMPORTANT: DO NOT DRINK. YET.). This draft you are going to want to type into a computer, and then email it to a stranger. You have to do this part. Wait, you are not done yet. Write about the whole experience on the outside of a winebottle and then drink the wine on the moon and sing a song about the color blue. This song you must memorize, etch into stone, and never breathe a word of to anyone. Now you are ready for step two: doing laundry. Write a poem on every item of clothing. Use a nonindelible crayon. At the laundromat, copy these poems onto gessoed 3-foot square (round will do equally well) canvases using alizarin crimson and vermilion oil paint thinned with a mixture of linseed oil and saliva. As you do this, put each item of clothing into the washing machine and consider the following: this is only the wash cycle, and the leaves reveal a shocking spectra as each bursts into flame and falls to rejoin the mud. The way I feel right now, before the rinse and spin, should be bottled and served on transatlantic flights to very sad businesspeople or Iceland. The suds you feel are irritating but they serve a purpose. There is no way to reverse any of these processes. The next stage is much more difficult. You must find a cafe whose owner agrees to let you have an art opening where you display your laundry paintings and walk among the guests as if you were one of the dead. This is the uncomfortable part but if you see it through then the gears are in motion. I have always wondered what it is like to speak in a conventional language and the other night when, fleeing human contact, I ran into you, I was unable to discourse. Someone spoke of dreamboats. That wasn't what I was talking about, although I said nothing. You see, something has been bothering me, *gnawing*, if you will, *at me*, and there is no way to say it to no one at no time no way, so I avoid the spoken word. Spoken word. Why do you think. When you say some things, do they cease to become true. It is like the tree

25

falling in a forest makes a noise *only if there is no person there to hear it*. Otherwise it is the person who is making the noise, internally, constructing the noise from the raw materials the falling tree provided; the creative act was that of the person hearing the tree fall. What were they doing in the woods anyway? If it were me, they would have said that I couldn't see the trees for the forest, but they would have been wrong. I am not like that. I see the trees. And I want to lie under them all. Each. Which, mathematically, is scarcely feasible. Which reminds me: people are often nice to each other. There are isolated occasions of interpersonal heroism. They are not to be criticized, or to be treated suspiciously, or seen as fitting into a larger and irresponsible pattern, but nurtured. Then, as you move your clothing to the dryer, write your last will and testament beginning with the words simply "I, _____, being of mind and body...." No one will hear the sound for the forest. For this reason, the only work you will do in the world is the work you are not paid for, all of which can reasonably and fairly be called art. Ready?

Up Go

my silly hopes again
now I would have given
hard to come by
circumstances are
you might like me in the right
man, I can imagine
I thought I was a good
time has passed more quickly than
have to fight off men all the
I love women

She Exists

within a radius of joy which
leaves none untouched leaves none
except intertwined in her hair
or found in pockets with twigs broken
bramble the love she collects
lost fingers of trees and drying leaves

flowers grope for her ankles and she runs
barefoot among vines dividing the grass
hoppers which she brings in with
her shoeless and mudtipped toes
encrusted with earth and jewelry
human pottery she dances
aflame with vision keeping
men away a fiery radius
in the uncombed thought
of prairie

the birds will reply idly to her cry
keep their time for themselves

The Tango Problem

The universe is composed of music
More complex and lovely than we can know

Let me take you across the floor
On this chariot of formal logic
Meteorites, fireflies tracing a deliberate math

And in this manner
Pass through one another
Each into the mirror emerges as its reflection

The city is large and elegant
Thriving and functional
Beneath it is a layer of compacted trash
A layer of mistakes held in place
By the weight of those
Who inhabit the consequences

The tango is a sun
That makes the earth transparent
Melts the trash into glass
Our sadness rising into a posture of dignity
We dance with our regrets, fears, despair
Reclaim them as our own, shards
Recontextualized as mosaic

Within me, my heart and lungs
In a shifting tempo

As you and I dance
We dance with the next couple
Circling in rhythm

I know nothing of you except your movement
As precise as water flowing over rocks
And now the music has ended
We part like strangers
You fall from my arms like the last leaf of autumn
Although you will now dance with a better man
I am dreamy, fulfilled

We dance with all life
As the earth with the moon (backleading)
The sun with other stars
The galaxy with other clusters
In a spiral of tango all the way out

Appositives

LAPD officers who terrorize African Americans should be
    taken off the street
LAPD officers, who terrorize African Americans, should be
    taken off the street

Weekdays when I stay in bed all day are the best
Weekdays, when I stay in bed all day, are the best

Military bases where sexual harassment takes place should be
    torn down
Military bases, where sexual harassment takes place, should be
    torn down

Reading how I have a sexuality is fun
Reading, how I have a sexuality, is fun

Reading why people lose their vision as they age is painful
Reading, why people lose their vision as they age, is painful

Violent rape is an atrocity
Violent, rape is an atrocity
Rape is violence
Violence is atrocity

War that is unnecessary is bad
War, which is unnecessary, is bad
Unnecessary war is bad
Unnecessary, war is bad

War is unnecessary
War is bad

That poetry that is political

Poetry, which is political

O'Ban

Watch the carnival of light stream through the platinum
    madness
The world inverted in the perfect curve of polished glass
Inhale the fumes, sinuses fiery, gasp, aghast with clarity
Bend over the snifter like an angel descending upon a lake of
    fire
Plunge your head into the madness, streaming bubbles
Come up sputtering, skin burning, being born
Shake your wings vigorously loosing droplets of golden poison
Spin in lazy circles, waterbug in warm June sun
Quit your job, divorce your wife, confess beauty, laugh at God
Wake up on the shore, gentle caress of flirtatious breeze
Pay the nice lady and don't forget your hat

Passive Voice

She would never be etched in stone. She would never be
published or written about. She would never even be
described. Immortality certainly not, and even the transience
of being mentioned would be cheerfully and finally refused.
Her files were stamped CONFIDENTIAL.

She was admitted in critical condition. She was treated and
nursed back to consciousness. From her first hazy moment of
awakening she was asked who had beaten her. Was he angered,
seduced, invited, talked into an extra drink, male? Had he
been employed by anyone, married to anyone, related to
anyone? Once he was identified, he would be apprehended,
put in custody, photographed, fingerprinted, questioned,
scrutinized, and examined. Who had battered her? She was
asked to identify him. They had to be told. She was wrapped in
more bandages than she felt necessary while being soothed,
sedated, sponged, sterilized, and squeezed for information.
A man like that, it was declared, was not to be trusted and
should be handed over. He had been raised wrong. He had
been accountable to no one and had been allowed to get away
with too much.

She was finally persuaded. He was apprehended. Their house
was searched. Evidence was turned up. Patients in her condition
are no longer admitted since Proposition 187 was passed.

Is Alright Everything Here?

The customer wasn't sure which of them was doing the other, the waitress or her job... the words "thank you" had stopped saying her and lousy service gave her to every table that waited on her all because a terrible tip got her written on a creditcard slip which took her to the customer whom the tip slowly erased using a ballpoint pen, then the credit card got the customer out of his wallet and took the waitress (who came by the table so he signaled her from across the room) to the computer which typed into her the amount they were going to pay the customer to produce his dinner, augmented by bones and lemonrind which at that moment used a hose to suck the dishwasher from the sink onto a plate which set him into a bustub which took him out to the waitress whose hands flew into the plate which took her to the customer whom the dinner then assembled in his stomach and mouth and set onto his plate with his fork while his waterglass emptied her into a pitcher, his ashtray replaced her with a dirty one, and the oily fingerprints removed the customer from the wineglass so it would have to smudge her later with her polishing cloth, so that a good waitress was her after rude was this customer to her so that the dinner, which finished him and took her to the kitchen, would take a long time separating the cooks into their constituent ingredients, and he waited an hour before his order took her but by then the lousy tip and rude behavior had forgotten her, remembering her with optimism, and, for months beforeward, peppermill before peppermill carried her from table before table and ground her all over the customers' salads.

That / Which

that box is a television, which is a form of language control
that you are susceptible to

which profits off the people it pays to work for it
that laid off 400,000 employees last year

which is the most exalted government position
that has managed so far to avoid jail

which is a form of language control
that you are susceptible to

which is an armed official whose job is to keep the peace
that is a brutal violent criminal

which is legal
that kills

which is the rule
that is the exception

which is intended to deter war and prevent death
that crashed during a practice bombing run killing all four crew
    members

which is your constitutional right
that is an incendiary, racist pamphlet distributed to those who
    did not solicit it

which means that the wealthy pay more
that is the exception

that is an unacceptable practice among politicians
which is the way the system works

which shows a slow decline in wealth for ninety percent of the
    population
that ten percent who is also the wealthiest ten percent

Autumn Poem

Strange, grey, tired, dust
Getting cold and smoky autumn
A gloomy congregation of stone buildings
Stand in the rain
A rough cold hurts the throat
The intersection of loneliness and exhaustion
It's dirty and cold and you can't close your eyes
Because opening them again would be too much work
Your own stupidity may be revealed in glimpses
Leaves, red, orange, yellow, green
Somewhere in you is a pod of flame
That says hope, fire, lust
Stones near a sundial, ashes
The fall of civilization, leaves, dusk
The last burn of sun, a thread of smoke
Until ice falls
Muscles brittle, bones ache
Mummify the splendor
Winter comes like static
Is there a limit to loneliness
The full moon asks to be a symbol of something
But its request lodges forgotten in a treetop
Eyelids of cast metal, your back hurts from staying awake
Dragging that brain around
Never did the mirror reflect you
In the evening time is like a river in that it cannot be slowed
Changes make little new
Oleanders underfoot
Leaving
Eternity = detritus

But

And I wanted to tell her my dream that she would be satisfied
with me / that the importance she ascribed to having an
actively nonmonogamous sexual life would fade / that in my
mind she would find a community as diverse as any / that in
my devotion was a freedom more sustainable than compulsive
promiscuity / in my hands would be revealed a new language
of gestures / in my alphabet were recombinant loveletters
yielding endless adaptive mutations / in my face were
dormant strangers waiting to emerge / in my voice
were the murmurs of crowds / in my behavior
were renunciations of cruelty / that hurting
a man wasn't feminism / that I had been
building / I had been
learning / had been
storing / was
ready / but

Keeping the Work Invisible

Once you are gone we vacuum the floors
Curse nursing burns behind steel doors
Throwing away what's left of your portion
Keeping the work invisible.

Expedite work from drawer to floor
Keep your appointments outside your door
Stubbornly poor we polish your fortune
Keeping the work invisible.

    And you'll never ask because
    We'll never let you
    You won't anticipate
    What we'll next get you
    Offered quite gently so
    Not to upset you
    We'll do the work so that
    You won't regret you.

(Before I undress the rest on your bedroom floors
My spermicide I apply behind bathroom doors
Apply it to mine though it applies more to yours
I'll roll on your condom you ignore my abortion
Which has kept certain work invisible.)

Keeping the work invisible.

Keeping the work indivisible.

Keeping the work invisible: yours.

Poem for Money I

Fill out applications by candlelight late at night with wine and Schubert. Do not answer the phone.	Write a story in the form of a detailed application for a part-time community college teaching position.
Fill out applications outdoors on beautiful days.	Make an oil painting eleven feet high and eight ½ feet wide which is a detailed reproduction of an application.
Fill out the application over and over until it's perfect.	Compose a piano piece by splicing together measures out of pieces teachers made you practice at some stage in your piano education in the order that you had to learn them.
If the interviewer ends a question on a middle C, what pitch should your answer end on?	Set an application to music.
Make a separate visit to a community college to deliver each document required with the application.	Reproduce the rectangles and proportions of an application onto a piece of watercolor paper.
Keep track of and recycle good answers to recurring application questions.	Try to make a copy of an application, word for word, by using words and letters cut out of books and magazines.
Try to apply for five jobs in one hour, whether they are jobs you want or not.	Walk to as many places as possible, collecting applications. The next day, return to them all and drop off the applications. Whether they are jobs you want or not.

Riskless (Metasestina)

Tell me fast: will a sestina break a picket line or even
end an even fast? Star a skyline? Will I break a sestina
open, taste a sestina, even with breakfast? Will I swallow a line
from a seven-line sestina? Will even a fast break
in a coffee break line jot a fast sestina? Or even a will?
I will break even. I line my coffin with a sestina fast.

I will not stand for an unemployment line. A lousy break.
I have no use for a sestina. Riskless, I even the odds fast.

Late to Work

I am the devil, asleep til 8:12.
I arrive late, fluorescence smothering
Here where the dry air never moves, I curse
Beauty. I stand at the water fountain
Measuring my sold life: antiseptic
Water, that fluid we are made of, my
Thoughts an angry chaos, bitter coffee.
Here where the walls are made of beige burlap
Sound-proof, light-proof, air-proof, thought-proof, riot-
Proof, tornado-proof, beauty-proof, me-proof.

I want to bang this job against the wall
Until it opens its eyes, sees itself.
I am not a slacker, but what difference?
Inert, drowning in salary, numb, dead.

Councilman Stumbles Home

In my dream you are waiting for me
In a white utopian landscape
Of uncomplicated public buildings.
It is Election Day and
You are wearing a purple scarf.
In the square we embrace
And share a kiss as slow and as lush as
Agriculture as the clock tower strikes
One thousand nine hundred and ninety-nine.

Now it is after closing time and
There is another blizzard.
In a swirling as white and relentless as paperwork,
I am lost and cannot find my Ward.
My preoccupied mind
Continually redistricting
This blank map.
Where is the grid beneath this
Tundra of unshoveled sidewalks?

Where is the
City salt for these locally-
Owned businesses?

Through unfamiliar alleyways
I leave tracks between fences
Where property owners sleep
Guarded by wary dogs I cannot name.

There is a constellation described
By certain points of this city:
The bulletin board outside the co-op
The newspapers at the Public Library
The clock opposite
The mailboxes median strips plazas
Brick streets and lampposts.

I have set my course by these stars
And wonder what, if any
Statement you are prepared to make.

Tonight you attended the meeting
But did not speak.
Leaving me afterward to collect
The shattered ruins
Of my briefcase. I was not always like this.
You were the one from my dream.
And you did not recognize me.

I once wore angry tshirts and was never without 1000
Signatures. All I could think about was
Military spending global warming and sex.
Now the sense of this Earth with which
I once took joy in organic gardening is in peril. I recycle
    diligently
But no longer own a tent or backpack.
Friendships stiffen into negotiations
I hear my name murmured in the mallmusic.

Blank newspapers blow through the decrepit
Business district of my heart
There is no one to subsidize a loan for renovation.

I spoke as well as I could
And I tipped the bartender
What I had calculated to be a living wage
But there is no satisfaction in any of it.

Where are you
My would-be constituent?

I clamber through these your snowdrifts
Your unplowed piles of frozen teardrops
A lost citizen.

East Timor

Question:
I am a "moderate" who is
"at heart benign." Who am
I?

Answer:
It's May 1998
and Madeline Albright's fingernail
wraps itself in the coils of the telephone
cord as she hisses a curse. Suharto takes
down his hat and leaves,
leaving the front door open.
A moment later the vice president
walks in wearing the same hat.

It's 1965
And our boys are running roughshod
over the PKI. You've seen Hitler, Stalin,
Mao, but you haven't seen the momentum
of history. One hundred thousand, "staggering,"
"a gleam of light in Asia." Get my
portfolio, it's almost time for the parade.

"Even
this small fragment of former
wealth came into the hands of
the rapacious stranger."

But don't fuck with the World
Bank. Don't try to screw the
IMF. Or we might call for
"a democratic transition."

It's 1975
and the great Portuguese empire
is beads scattering from a broken thread.
"Kissingerian realism."
Oil reserves + American
weapons = 200,000.
Indonesia took Timor,
Carter smiled, and the newspapers
were blank.

It's 1978
and the massacre in East Timor
is hitting its stride
into its third year.
European nations and America
creep in to tear off what hunks of
meat they can.

It's 1999
and the Timorese have voted
for independence. 75% of
the votes of 90% of the voters,
even under intimidation. A violence
even we would find unreal
is exploding. Indonesia considers
this their domestic affair and is keeping
the rest of the world at bay. "The
pioneer and exemplar for every kind of
atrocity." The Phoenix and the Contras,
arise, going after every last citizen.

Burning churches,
modern assault rifles,
babies,
razor wire,
continuous gunfire,
systematically.

31 January 1996 Los Angeles

Beneath this concrete double helix
I admire the development
That has brought the touch of elegance to my districts.

In cologne and silk
And fine leather hunting gear
Whose fine craftsmanship would mesmerize
Rabbits.

Shoveling the renovation
Of the twisted wreckage of the village
A villager with a tie of links
Who eyes the applecore by the side of the boulevard
And eyes the guard
And eyes the applecore by the side of the boulevard.

The drumming is getting louder than the tinkling of ice in the
    glasses.

You Never Thanked the Poor

A soft life made you hard, you grew a shell
But who's that singing songs outside your door
They're here because you never thanked the poor
The ones who let you live so very well

Go to the door, I hear the bell
Now is your chance to thank the poor
Civilization's compressed core
In Mozambique and Ecuador
In East Timor and Baltimore
The Philippines and Salvador
In Harlem, Watts, and Singapore
Who stitched each shoe you ever wore
Who built your car, who clean your floor
Who stock your food, who run your store
Who guard your prisons, fight your war
So sweaty starving stiff and sore
Whose labor is an awful chore
A torturous, godawful bore
Your pastry chef and stevedore
Your longshoreman and furthermore
Your pastor, proctor, professor
Conductor, author, commodore
Mortician, coroner and more
Are here to hear the words you tell

Them when you hear the words they yell

You never thanked the poor
Who let you live that way
You never thanked the poor
Who let you live that long
You never thanked

The poor who let
You live

Friday Poem

Last night in a dream I asked someone, *am I being detained or am I free to go?*

Just because your worst fears weren't realized doesn't mean things are all that great

It will take them an excruciatingly long time to retract their kind offer unexpectedly

Who said you have to finish every single notebook? tear out the pages

Sometimes when you ask people to give you things for free they don't respond

When they told you how much it would cost to fix the problem went away

In most cases it wouldn't kill people to be more considerate of one another

Only a coward would hide from a birthday party

How do you feel when a bad thing and a good thing happen at the same time

Is it better if the good thing happens more quickly than the bad thing? or worse

Busy getting ready to do nothing all weekend

How does one sense when one is not sensitive enough

Confusion is natural, apathy is social

You can learn about yourself from what you are afraid will
happen, if it doesn't

I don't read much theory lately; I've been reading nonfiction

Sometimes everything goes wrong; this is to be expected and
welcomed

Ladies

Young man, don't you think you're a little
young to be calling in sick twice
in one month? What are you? Twenty-
nine? Young thing like you. Ever hear of medicine?
Do we look healthy to you, son? Listen

Let your little girl aspirations dissolve like a spoonful
of saccharin in Sanka. Our children also crave
freedom and we resent them for it. Look in my pocketbook
Tampax, Kleenex, Valium, Tums
a panoply of pharmaceuticals
anesthetic casserole. I remember my third month too
when you can first feel the fluorescence
beginning to dissolve the edges of your brain
you acquire a new stutter and an appetite for network
television. Oh yes, you have sat on your modular sofa
with death and found it disturbingly comfortable.

Look at these disembowled matriarchs
each arrives with a meticulous flourish
approaching the same stairway following the same
footprints each morning everytime like the same
robotic ambassador or the same
fossilized weapons inspector envoy
each bearing with her her own
quaint curious anachronistic idiosyncratic
luncheon rituals and patterns of interaction
elaborate pantomimes in a soporific compromise
life the animal with its slime and tendrils and teeth
now reduced to a humming box of light
from the hour when the sun is cracked on the horizon
drooling its warm yolk into the upturned beaks of shrieking
    birds

to the hour when the parks are reclaimed by hideous
possums and narcissistic raccoons.

You span these hours riding an ergonomic swivelchair
losing ground against the slippery slope
of the asymptotic curve of information storage and retrieval
and the shifting, diminishing dunes of the job market
far from its theoretical limits, while you hold court
in a pit of overflowing file folders the person who
had this office before you didn't throw out because
the person before her didn't throw them out.

And it is at precisely this hour when the coffee
sparks in you a cornucopia of inspiration snaking
vines sprouting flowers of ideas
but you know that this enthusiasm too shall pass
and the warm pleasure of obsolescence
is a shot of poison in your arm
as you pivot taking it all in
locked in the safedepositbox of a secure income
your future a long soft white shimmering tunnel
of health insurance counting the dollars between
CATscans.

56   How many times will you return to this same waterfountain
whose water and your blood are intermingled, synonymous
going through motions in this harsh flickering pageant
in a mannequin mimicry of gesture and inflection
in this sexless hospital of our collectively curtailed intentions
a bureaucratic masquerade drifting through the atrium
chit-chatting across a desert the color of bone drained of all
    cocktails
each one a scarred rib in the skeleton of a dead dinosaur
conducting research for teachers who would be better suited
with bulletproof vests.

You think you don't feel well, well
you should spend a day in my arthritic apparatus
these tendons a map of inflammation
pentium flakes embedded in my skin.

We are all mutilated in this office
having hacked off limbs to fit through the doorway
now amputated adult stillbirths of capitalist patriarchy
we huddle in this aquarium, our limbs twisted and paralytic
squatting before humming machines
we watch the sun through a microscope slide set high on the
        wall
our lifetimes piling up like forms in an overflowing outbasket.

I am little more spontaneous then a wristwatch
slackening, unwinding, losing power
on a wrist that keeps shaking until well into the second chablis
and yet marking the seconds with uncanny precision
biorhythms wired to a punchclock.

Our husbands are tenured
numb in their indifferent scholarship
bored mumbling through halitosis lecturehalls
until their next application of the nametag
at the next conference in Syracuse
to accept the award—winner of the Salt
Hill hypertext contest—and an evening spent drinking
tequila with colleague Jeff Parker bullshitting about
Derrida and Hobbes.

A cascade of manila folders dry like dead sycamore leaves
rustling across the rheumatoid afternoon.
A bone spur of deflated sleep.
I've recoiled enough from a glimpse
of a life of freedom and would prefer
two weeks in the Bermuda islands.

A shipwrecked tanker on a TV schedule
age has dealt me two heavy blows:

1. My teeth
2. A complicated affair involving iodine and urinalysis

My childhood traumas intact and stored in
a stable directory structure. It cleanses me
this umbilical between me and this computer
with its angles and desktop publishing software
its unstable mechanisms no more arcane than my own.

I experience the world through an
inflamed carpal tunnel, diarrhea, and
a distant toothache. These #s and %s. 200 MHz & above.

But I have good days too.

A parade of tiny children carrying big clipboards
shuffles past my door. They are bespectacled and
inventorying fire extinguishers. May this ibuprofen blunt
me for sweeps week. This springtime of my
undertaking. Having earned in this respect a trifle
measure of the privilege allotted me by my
station. I understand how the personality is
like a gyroscope, intensely stable if anchored by
a single point. I am middle-aged and may shift from rinse
to spin anytime.

There is weather on my veranda.
There has been a train collision in my heart.
And in my mind another high school murderer.

I sure hope you feel better young man
by tomorrow, and we will cheerfully
interrogate you in the morning breakroom.

You see, we are all sick.
And we come to work on time.

Feta and Tofu

Should I plan
on living near you or plan
around living near you or plan
despite living near you or plan
by living near you?

If
if if
if if if
if if if if
if if if if if I could write you a text that wouldn't poison itself
with selfcategorization like a mobius scorpion, then I would
flow through it towards you pseunami tsudopod engulfing
infiltrating loving you and through you and around you and
over you and under you. If text weren't art weren't history
weren't a battle between victors and omissions who were erased
in two thousand quiet conflicts in the smoke of which
interpretations were erected and taught to say "we were here all
along, we were here all along...," if I weren't stumbling through
a ruined slum of precedents, then I could function within a
sentence without situating myself on a critic's grid or a
spectrum or circle or on one side of a twosided object and I
would lick all your skin off with the curve of my period. If the
play of the letters didn't refer to two thousand recognizable
patterns and the play of words didn't suggest two thousand
preexisting tangents, if it all wasn't a ready-made vocabulary,
paintbox, toybox, toolbox, if it were strawberries and

butterflies and I were the sun, then my commas would be tangled in your hair while I gently chewed your ligaments. If I were memorizing every circular inch of your skin with a lip or fingernail, if I were tasting you everywhere, if we took turns being inside one another, if I could touch the shufflethump of your heart with this trembling erection, then this couldn't be a letter story poem play essay manifesto shoppinglist will and testament. If any of this were real before or after language, if only language rose in the east and set in the west, if only I weren't writing this, if it were me and you were you and I touched your nose and whispered a rainbow of flavors and vitamins and basted your membranes with my nutritional saliva until your skin rose orange like warm cinnamon, if you had orgasms in every organ at once and burst into flames and continued living happily on fire, then I would come banana milkshakes and drool olive oil and sweat lime and coat you with my secretions until you were warm and slippery then wrap myself all the way around you until you couldn't see out and could hear nothing but my purring and then retract and curl up between your thighs wrapping my tail in a spiral all the way down your leg and flex and relax and flex and relax while I tickled your foot with my dry stinger then exhale my left lung into your vagina and blow until the tickling of two thousand microscopic alveolar sacs rendered your cranium a tangled roadmap of warm lakes and beaches then straddle your stomach and regurgitate pure chocolate into your mouth until I were panting damp and exhausted with my thumb in your bellybutton caressing the curve of your appendix and my

forefinger in your ear touching your most pleasant memories.
Even if I could display atomic time and phase of the moon,
indicate temperature and humidity, even if I could pick up
police radios, even if I approached the theoretical limit of
information transmission, even if I spoke two thousand
languages, even if I could encrypt a library in one
twothousandth of a second, then I would
rather we come until we were all gone
and the carpet was soaked.

There could have been two thousand pronouns for you.
When we see us we will link tongues and teach each other
to touch so slowly the days will flicker past the window.

Death of the St. Pauli Girl

I had no light at the end of the tunnel
I had no tunnel
I was buried

My bones rattled as ice
Dissolving in the scotch
Of the earth

Now the light at the end
Of my tunnel
Is each day's setting sun

Until dawn's bottlecap
Pried loose
Hisses a foam of birdsong

Acknowledgements

"With Shoes Like These" was published in *Druid's Cave* and *Black Dirt*. "Little Villainelle" was published in *Druid's Cave*. "Static of Baghdad," "Newspoem 5 January 1995," "The Week The News Was Put in Prison," "Late to Work," "Councilman Stumbles Home," "East Timor," "31 January 1996 Los Angeles," "You Never Thanked the Poor," and "Ladies" were published on *Newspoetry* (newspoetry.com). "Conjecture and Proposition," "Little Villainelle," "Up Go," "But," "Keeping the Work Invisible," and "Riskless (Metasestina)," were published in *Table of Forms* (spinelessbooks.com/table). "Appositives," "Is Alright Everything Here?," "Passive Voice," and "That/Which" are from *Grammar Primer*. This survey of the millennial poetry of William Gillespie was edited with Stephanie Strickland, C.D. Scoggins, and Dirk Stratton.

Lost Citizen: Selected Poems 1995–2003, by William Gillespie
Second Spineless Edition 2008-02-20 © Spineless Books
ISBN 978-0-9801392-0-4 paper
Library of Congress Control Number: 2008900679
Cover art: Road Map to Creativity (excerpt)
© Scott Westgard (westgardfineart.net)

Spineless Books
PO Box 17191, Urbana, IL 61803
www.spinelessbooks.com

SPINELESS BOOKS, URBANA